The Modern Guide to Making Money Online: Unlocking Financial Freedom from Anywhere

Hope Judge

TABLE OF
CONTENTS

INTRODUCTION

The Promise of Online Income

An overview of how the internet has revolutionized personal finance, providing individuals with tools to create, promote, and sell their skills, products, and expertise. Discuss the importance of self-discipline, digital literacy, and the entrepreneurial mindset required for online success.

Types of Online Income Streams

Active Income: Income that requires ongoing work, like freelancing or remote employment. **Passive Income:** Income streams that earn money after an initial effort, such as digital products or affiliate marketing.

Identifying Your Goals

Help readers assess their current financial needs, time commitment, and personal strengths. This section will guide readers on setting SMART goals (Specific, Measurable, Achievable, Relevant, TimeBound) tailored to their online money-making journey.

CHAPTER I

GETTING STARTED WITH FREELANCING

Overview of Freelancing

Explain freelancing's advantages, including location flexibility, client variety, and income potential, as well as challenges like job instability and managing client expectations.

Identifying Your Skills

Break down popular freelance skills:
- **Writing and Content Creation**: For blog posts, copywriting, technical writing.
- **Graphic Design and Video Editing**: Skills like logo creation, animation, video production.
- **Programming and Tech Services**: Coding, app development, cybersecurity.
- **Virtual Assistance**: For clients who need help with administrative tasks.

CONTENT

Graphic Design and Video Editing

Writing and Content Creation

HTML/CSS

JS

PHP

Virtual Assistance

Programming and Tech Services

Freelance Platforms Overview

Detailed breakdown of freelance marketplaces:

- **Upwork:** Ideal for various professional services, tips on building a strong profile, navigating the bidding system.
- **Fiverr:** How to create "gigs," optimize descriptions, and establish gig extras.
- **Freelancer and Toptal:** Understanding their strengths, fee structures, and clientele.

Upwork

Fiverr

Freelancer

Toptal

Building a Profile That Stands Out

Showcase how to:

- Write a bio that highlights unique skills.
- Create a portfolio with examples or case studies, even if they're mock projects.

Securing Your First Job

Strategies for setting beginner-friendly rates, writing effective proposals, and securing testimonials.

Scaling Your Freelance Business

Discuss advanced strategies, like pricing your services competitively, building client relationships, and outsourcing smaller tasks.

CHAPTER 2

E-COMMERCE AND DROPSHIPPING

Understanding E-commerce and Dropshipping

Explore how e-commerce and dropshipping differ from traditional retail, and why each can be profitable with relatively low upfront costs.

Setting Up Your Store

Platform Selection

- **Shopify**: Perfect for beginners, user-friendly, integrates with dropshipping apps.
- **WooCommerce**: Ideal for users familiar with WordPress, high customizability.
- **Etsy**: A platform for handmade, vintage items, and unique products.

Shopify

WooCommerce

Etsy

Finding Products to Sell

- **Product Research:** Using tools like Google Trends, Amazon Bestsellers, and Oberlo.
- **Sourcing and Dropshipping:** Exploring options through AliExpress, Alibaba, and using local suppliers.

Marketing Your E-commerce Store

Step-by-step guide on setting up:

- **SEO for E-commerce:** Optimizing product titles, descriptions, and images.
- **Social Media Marketing:** Content ideas for Instagram, TikTok, and Facebook Ads.
- **Influencer Partnerships:** Reaching out to micro-influencers to awareness.

Scaling and Automating Your Business

Using apps and software for inventory management, customer service bots, email marketing automation, and scaling using paid ads.

CHAPTER 3

AFFILIATE MARKETING AND CONTENT CREATION

What is Affiliate Marketing?

How affiliate marketing works and how it can turn content creation into a sustainable revenue stream.

Choosing a Niche and Platform

Steps to research niches by exploring competitor websites, Google Keyword Planner, and popular categories on affiliate networks.

Building Your Audience

Platform-specific content strategies:

- **Blogging:** Regular, valuable content optimized for search engines.

- **affiliate marketing YouTube:** Tutorials, product reviews, and unboxing videos.
- **Instagram/TikTok:** Visual content, storytelling, and partnering with brands.

Selecting the Right Affiliate Programs

Overview of affiliate platforms like:

Amazon Associates: Ideal for physical products, suitable for beginner bloggers.
ShareASale and CJ Affiliate: Great for established brands, higher commission rates.

Effective Content Marketing for Conversions

Tips for driving traffic that converts:
- Use clear Calls-to-Action (CTAs).
- Include personal experiences to build trust.

Tracking and Scaling Your Income

Tools for tracking conversions, like Google Analytics, affiliate dashboards, and tips on using A/B testing to improve conversion rates.

CHAPTER 4
DIGITAL PRODUCTS AND
ONLINE COURSES

The Appeal of Digital Products

Explain the benefits of selling e-books, online courses, templates, etc., as an income model that generates passive revenue.

Choosing the Right Product

How to identify product ideas by:

- Surveying your audience.
- Looking at what competitors offer.
- Validating the demand through presales or social media.

Platforms for Hosting Digital Products

Breakdown of platform pros and cons:

- **Gumroad:** Great for artists and small businesses.
- **Teachable/Udemy:** Well-suited for online courses, easy-to-use with large audiences.
- **Amazon Kindle Direct Publishing:** Ideal for aspiring authors and e-book creators.

Building Your Product

Guidance on writing an e-book, creating course content (videos, worksheets), and producing templates or other digital downloads.

Marketing and Launch Strategies

Creating a launch strategy:

- Use email marketing, SEO, and paid ads.
- Leverage early customer reviews to increase credibility.

Managing Feedback and Scaling

Importance of gathering user feedback, making improvements, and creating related products to expand offerings.

CHAPTER 5

BLOGGING AND SEO MONETIZATION

Starting Your Blog

Detailed guide on setting up a blog, choosing a niche, and using tools like WordPress or Squarespace.

Content Creation Strategies

- **Keyword Research**: Using tools like Ahrefs, Ubersuggest, and SEMrush.
- **Content Planning**: Creating topic clusters, maintaining posting consistency.

SEO Fundamentals

Introduction to on-page and off-page SEO, backlinking, and user experience optimization.

Monetizing Your Blog

Strategies for earning revenue:

- **Ad Networks:** Google AdSense and MediaVine for display ads.
- **Sponsored Content:** Reaching out to brands and structuring fair deals.

- **Affiliate Links:** Incorporating affiliate marketing.

Long-Term Growth and Diversification

Expand a blog into a full brand by creating products, adding a podcast, or consulting.

CHAPTER 6

STOCK PHOTOGRAPHY AND VIDEO CONTENT

Howto Get Started in Stock Photography /Videography

Overview of the demand for stock photography, especially for digital marketing, advertising, and website design.

Creating High-Quality Content

Photography tips, including lighting, composition, editing basics, and equipment recommendations.

Choosing What to Shoot

Identifying high-demand niches, like lifestyle, office settings, nature, and abstract backgrounds.

Uploading and Tagging Your Work

Best practices for uploading, using relevant keywords, and maximizing exposure on platforms like Shutterstock and Adobe Stock.

Earning Royalties and Scaling

Discuss the payout structure and strategies for increasing earnings through video content or exclusive stock agreements.

CHAPTER 7

REMOTE WORK AND VIRTUAL ASSISTANCE

Overview of Virtual Assistance

A VA'sjob, covering tasks such as managing social media, customer support, and handling administrative work.

Identifying Your Skill Set

List of potential VA tasks, including appointment scheduling, social media posting, and basic bookkeeping.

Setting Up as a VA

Guide on finding clients through LinkedIn, Facebook groups, and VA-specific sites like Belay and Time etc.

Pricing Your Services

Explanation of hourly vs. package rates, common price ranges, and methods for pricing based on skills.

Scaling Your VA Business

Building an agency by hiring other VAs, creating service packages, and establishing client contracts.

CHAPTER 8

SIDE HUSTLES IN THE GIG ECONOMY

Survey Websites and Microtasks

Quick gigs on Swagbucks, Pinecone Research, and TaskRabbit.

Testing Websites and Apps

Howto earn by testing products on platforms like User Testing, TryMyUI, and Respondent.io.

Cashback and Rewards Programs

Using apps like Rakuten, Honey, and Ibotta for cash-back savings.

CHAPTER 9
MANAGING AND SCALING YOUR ONLINE INCOME

Budgeting for Freelancers and Entrepreneurs

Budgeting on a fluctuating income, understanding taxes, and emergency funds.

Investing Your Earnings

Basic principles of reinvesting in your business, long-term investing, and diversification of income streams.

Networking and Personal Branding

Building a reputation, engaging with other professionals on LinkedIn, and using social media for networking.

CHAPTER 10

MASTERING AUTOMATION FOR PASSIVE INCOME

The Role of Automation in Online Business

Automation is the cornerstone of scaling an online business while freeing up time. By leveraging tools and systems, entrepreneurs can minimize manual tasks and focus on growth strategies.

Areas Where Automation Works Best

- **E-commerce:** Tools like Shopify and Oberlo automate inventory management and order fulfillment.
- **Email Marketing:** Platforms like Mailchimp or ConvertKit enable pre-scheduled campaigns and personalized outreach.
- **Social Media Management:** Tools like Hootsuite and Buffer schedule posts, monitor engagement, and analyze performance.

Key Automation Tools

- **Zapier:** Connects apps to automate repetitive tasks, like syncing sales data with spreadsheets.
- **IFTTT (If This, Then That):** Automates workflows across apps, such as saving social media mentions to a task list.

Key Automation Tools

- **Chatbots:** Tools like ManyChat enhance customer interaction by providing 24/7 support.

Benefits of Automation

- Increases efficiency and reduces operational costs.
- Improves customer experience through faster response times.
- Enhances scalability by enabling businesses to handle more tasks simultaneously.

Implementation Tips

Start small by automating repetitive tasks, then expand to more complex processes as your business grows. Prioritize tools that align with your current business model and goals.

BUILDING AN ONLINE COMMUNITY

Why Online Communities Matter

Building a strong online community fosters trust, engagement, and loyalty among your audience. A connected group of followers can amplify your reach, provide valuable feedback, and even become your most enthusiastic advocates.

Areas Where Automation Works Best

- **E-commerce:** Tools like Shopify and Oberlo automate inventory management and order fulfillment.
- **Email Marketing:** Platforms like Mailchimp or ConvertKit enable pre-scheduled campaigns and personalized outreach.
- **Social Media Management:** Tools like Hootsuite and Buffer schedule posts, monitor engagement, and analyze performance.

Strategies for Engagement

- **Content Sharing**: Post-value-driven content such as tutorials, webinars, or exclusive offers.
- **Interactive Activities**: Host live Q&A sessions, polls, and contests to keep members involved.
- **Encourage Collaboration**: Allow members to share their experiences, advice, or creations.

Monetizing Your Community

- Offer premium memberships for exclusive access to content.
- Use affiliate links and sponsored posts within the group.
- Organize workshops or sell products tailored to the group's interests.

Sustaining Growth

Consistency is key. Regular updates, active moderation, and genuine interaction will ensure the community thrives.

BUILDING A REMOTE TEAM FOR SUCCESS

The Remote Work Revolution

The shift to remote work has enabled businesses to tap into a global talent pool, reduce overhead costs, and enhance flexibility. Success in building a remote team lies in strategic hiring, effective management, and fostering cohesion despite geographical barriers.

Hiring the Right Talent

- **Define Roles Clearly:** Create detailed job descriptions outlining responsibilities and required skills.
- **Global Platforms:** Use platforms like Upwork, Remote.co, and LinkedIn to find international talent.
- **Assess Compatibility:** Beyond technical skills, evaluate candidates' ability to work

- autonomously and communicate effectively in a virtual environment.

Effective Team Management

- **Set Expectations:** Establish clear goals, deadlines, and communication norms.
- **Leverage Technology:** Use tools like Slack for messaging, Asana for project management, and Zoom for virtual meetings.
- **Track Progress:** Regularly review performance through weekly check-ins and measurable KPIs.

Fostering Cohesion and Productivity

- Build Relationships: Encourage informal chats or virtual coffee breaks to strengthen team bonds.
- Celebrate Wins: Recognize achievements publicly to motivate team members.
- Adapt Flexibility: Respect cultural differences and accommodate varying time zones to promote inclusivity.

Scaling Your Team

- Structured Onboarding: Implement a standardized onboarding process to integrate new hires smoothly.
- Knowledge Sharing: Use shared drives or tools like Notion to maintain accessible resources.

- **Encourage Feedback:** Create an open feedback culture to continuously improve processes and engagement.

CHAPTER 13

LEVERAGING AI FOR ONLINE INCOME

The Power of AI in Digital Businesses

Artificial Intelligence (AI) is revolutionizing the way online income streams are managed and optimized. By integrating AI tools, entrepreneurs can automate complex tasks, enhance customer experiences, and gain data-driven insights to scale operations effectively.

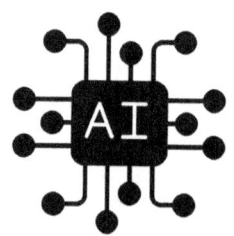

AI Applications in Earning Online

- **Content Creation:** Tools like ChatGPT and Jasper generate blog posts, product descriptions, and ad copies.
- **Customer Support:** Chatbots powered by AI, such as ManyChat or Intercom, provide 24/7 assistance, improving customer satisfaction.
- **Market Analysis:** Platforms like SEMrush and MarketMuse use AI to analyze competition and identify profitable niches.

- **E-commerce Personalization:** AI-driven recommendation engines increase sales by suggesting relevant products to customers.

Getting Started with AI Tools

- **Budget-Friendly Options:** Start with free AI tools like Canva for graphic design or Google Analytics for data insights.
- **Advanced Solutions:** Invest in platforms like HubSpot for comprehensive marketing automation or Looker Studio for advanced analytics.

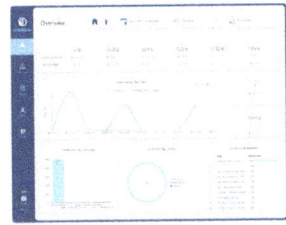

Future Trends

AI's role will only expand. Emerging fields like generative design, voice commerce, and predictive analytics offer untapped potential for online entrepreneurs.

Tips for Success

Start small by automating repetitive tasks, then gradually adopt AI for strategic decision-making and scaling operations.

CHAPTER 14

CRYPTOCURRENCY AND BLOCKCHAIN OPPORTUNITIES

Understanding Cryptocurrency and Blockchain
Cryptocurrency, such as Bitcoin and Ethereum, represents a revolutionary digital asset class that operates on blockchain technology. Blockchain is a decentralized, transparent ledger system that enables secure transactions without intermediaries.

Earning Opportunities in Cryptocurrency

- **Trading and Investing**: Buy, sell, and hold cryptocurrencies to capitalize on market fluctuations.
- **Mining**: Earn rewards by validating transactions and securing the blockchain network.
- **Staking**: Lock your crypto assets in a wallet to support blockchain operations and earn rewards.

- **NFT Creation and Sales:** Use platforms like OpenSea to design and sell Non-Fungible Tokens, catering to art, music, and collectibles.

Blockchain-Based Careers

- **Smart Contract Development:** Creating automated agreements on platforms like Ethereum.
- **Decentralized Finance (DeFi):** Participating in lending and borrowing through decentralized platforms.

Getting Started

- Use trusted exchanges like Binance or Coinbase for buying cryptocurrencies.
- Learn blockchain basics through free resources like Binance Academy or Coursera.

Future Trends

Blockchain technology is expanding into fields like real estate, supply chain management, and gaming.

Staying updated ensures long-term success in this dynamic sector.

CHAPTER 15

BECOMING A SOCIAL MEDIA INFLUENCER

The Rise of Short-Form Content

Platforms like TikTok, YouTube Shorts, and Instagram Reels have revolutionized content consumption. These short, engaging videos capture attention quickly, making them ideal for aspiring influencers to build a following.

Building Your Personal Brand

- **Define Your Niche:** Focus on areas like fitness, travel, food, or tech to attract a specific audience.
- **Consistency is Key:** Post regularly to maintain engagement. Aim for 3–5 uploads per week.
- **Optimize Profiles:** Use professional bios, clear profile pictures, and links to websites or other social platforms.

Content Creation Tips

- **Engaging Videos:** Keep videos short, visually appealing, and aligned with trending hashtags or sounds.
- **Authenticity:** Showcase your unique personality to connect with your audience.
- **Leverage Tools:** Use in-app editing tools, filters, and text overlays to enhance your videos.

Monetizing Your Platform

- **Sponsored Posts:** Partner with brands to promote products or services.
- **Affiliate Marketing:** Share affiliate links to earn a commission on sales.
- **Creator Funds:** Join programs like TikTok Creator Fund or YouTube Partner Program for revenue sharing.
- **Product Sales:** Sell merchandise or offer services like consultations directly.

Growing Your Influence

Engage with followers through comments, live sessions, and collaborations with other influencers to expand your reach.

CHAPTER 16

GAMING FOR PROFIT

The Rise of Gaming as a Career

Gaming has evolved beyond a recreational activity to a profitable career path. Platforms like Twitch, YouTube Gaming, and the Unity Asset Store have provided opportunities for gamers to earn substantial income through various avenues.

Building Your Gaming Brand

- **Focus on a Niche:** Specialize in genres like first-person shooters, RPGs, or strategy games to attract a dedicated audience.
- **Consistency is Key:** Stream regularly or create a portfolio of assets to maintain visibility in the gaming community.
- **Engaging Profiles:** Optimize profiles on platforms like Twitch or asset marketplaces with professional branding and detailed descriptions.

Profitable Avenues in Gaming

1. Streaming on Twitch

- **Subscriptions:** Earn revenue from viewers subscribing to your channel for exclusive perks.
- **Donations and Bits:** Receive direct support from your audience during live streams.
- **Ad Revenue and Sponsorships:** Partner with brands or run ads to generate income.

2. Selling Game Assets

- **What to Sell:** Characters, environments, textures, or animations.
- **Platforms:** Use marketplaces like Unity Asset Store or GameDev Market to reach buyers.
- **Tools for Creation:** Design assets using Blender, Maya, or Photoshop.

3. Coaching Players

- **What to Offer:** Train players in competitive games or help teams improve collaboration.
- **Where to Start:** Platforms like GamerSensei connect coaches with aspiring players.
- **Build Your Reputation:** Tailor coaching strategies to meet the individual needs of players.

Growing Your Influence

Engage with your audience by:
- Engage with your audience by:Hosting live Q&A sessions or gameplay tutorials.
- Collaborating with other gamers or streamers.
- Sharing behind-the-scenes content to build a personal connection.

Conclusion

Gaming for profit is a dynamic field with multiple opportunities. By leveraging platforms, building a personal brand, and engaging with your audience, you can transform your passion for gaming into a sustainable income source.

CHAPTER 17

ONLINE TUTORING AND COACHING

How to Turn Your Expertise into an Educational Side Hustle

The Rise of Online Tutoring

With the increasing demand for flexible learning, online tutoring has emerged as a lucrative side hustle. Platforms like Wyzant, TutorMe, and Preply allow educators to connect with students worldwide, offering knowledge on a range of topics.

Building Your Online Tutoring Brand

- **Identify Your Niche**: Specialize in subjects you excel at, such as math, languages, or coding.
- **Define Your Audience**: Decide whether to target school students, college learners, or working professionals.
- **Optimize Your Online Presence**: Create professional profiles on tutoring platforms or build a website with clear descriptions of your services.

Steps to Get Started

- **Set Up the Basics:** Use tools like Zoom for virtual lessons and Canva for creating promotional materials.
- **Design a Curriculum:** Break down topics into manageable lessons with clear goals.
- **Offer Value:** Provide free introductory sessions to showcase your teaching style.

Monetizing Your Expertise

- **One-on-One Tutoring:** Charge hourly rates for personalized lessons.
- **Pre-Recorded Courses:** Develop reusable content to sell on platforms like Udemy.
- **Group Workshops:** Host seminars or interactive classes for multiple learners.

Engaging and Retaining Clients

- Use feedback to refine your lessons.
- Maintain consistent communication with students and parents.
- Offer flexible scheduling to accommodate diverse time zones.

Conclusion

Online tutoring is an excellent way to monetize your expertise while making a meaningful impact. By providing quality education and leveraging online tools, you can create a sustainable side hustle that grows with time.

CHAPTER 18

FRANCHISE-LIKE ONLINE BUSINESSES

Exploring Models like Print-on-Demand or Subscription-Based Services

The Rise of Franchise-Like Online Businesses

Franchise-like models in the online space, such as Print-on-Demand (POD) and subscription-based services, provide opportunities for entrepreneurs to scale businesses without handling physical inventory or significant overhead costs. These models blend the flexibility of e-commerce with the reliability of franchising.

Building Your Franchise-Like Business

- **Choose Your Niche:** Focus on specific products like fitness gear, custom apparel, or educational resources.
- **Select the Right Platform:** Use platforms like Shopify, WooCommerce, or Etsy to host your store.

- **Optimize Branding**: Develop a professional brand identity with a memorable logo and consistent messaging.

Exploring Models

1. Print-on-Demand (POD)

- **How It Works**: Create custom designs that are printed on items like T-shirts, mugs, or notebooks when an order is placed.
- **Key Platforms**: Printful, Gelato, and Printify.
- **Benefits**: No upfront inventory costs and low risk.

2. Subscription-Based Services

- **How It Works**: Charge recurring fees for ongoing access to a product or service, such as curated subscription boxes or digital content.
- **Key Examples**: Netflix for streaming, or subscription meal kits.
- **Benefits**: Predictable revenue streams and high customer retention.

Steps to Monetize Your Model

- **Market Your Products:** Use SEO, social media ads, and influencer partnerships to reach your audience.
- **Upsell and Retain:** Offer premium tiers or exclusive products to boost recurring revenue.
- **Leverage Analytics:** Use tools like Google Analytics or Shopify Insights to track performance and refine strategies.

Conclusion

Franchise-like online business models like POD and subscription-based services are scalable, profitable, and ideal for modern entrepreneurs. By combining creativity with strategic planning, you can establish a sustainable and flexible source of income.

CHAPTER 19

INTERNATIONAL MARKETS

The Importance of International Markets

Expanding to global markets enables businesses to access larger customer bases, diversify income streams, and strengthen brand presence. The rise of e-commerce and digital tools has made entering international markets more accessible than ever.

Building Your Global Presence

- **Research Market Opportunities:** Study demand trends, purchasing power, and competitive landscapes in target regions.
- **Cultural Adaptation:** Tailor your products, services, and marketing strategies to align with local preferences and customs.
- **Leverage Technology:** Use platforms like Shopify and Amazon for e-commerce and

tools like Google Translate to bridge language gaps.

Strategies for Success in Global Markets

1. Selling Services or Products

- **E-commerce Platforms:** Sell directly through platforms like Amazon, Alibaba, or Etsy.
- **Localization:** Adjust pricing, packaging, and messaging to meet regional expectations.

2. Cross-Cultural Collaboration

- **Understand Cultural Nuances:** Learn about local business etiquette, communication styles, and decision-making processes.
- **Diverse Teams:** Collaborate with local experts or hire a diverse team to gain insights into cultural preferences.

3. Build Trust

- **Transparency in Policies:** Clearly communicate shipping policies, returns, and customer support.
- **Customer Support:** Offer multilingual support to cater to a global audience.

Expanding Your Market

Entering international markets requires agility and a commitment to learning. By leveraging cross-cultural insights and digital tools, businesses can thrive in the global economy while fostering meaningful international relationships.

CHAPTER 20

UPSKILLING WITH FREE AND PAID RESOURCES

The Importance of Upskilling

As the job market evolves, acquiring high-income skills like coding, copywriting, and video editing has become essential. These skills open doors to lucrative opportunities in freelancing, entrepreneurship, and traditional careers.

Building Your Learning Strategy

- **Define Your Goals:** Choose skills aligned with your career aspirations.
- **Mix Free and Paid Resources:** Balance free tools with structured paid courses for comprehensive learning.
- **Set a Learning Schedule:** Dedicate consistent time to skill-building each week.

Top Platforms for Learning High-Income Skills

1. Coding

- **Free Resources:** FreeCodeCamp, Codecademy (basic plan).
- **Paid Courses:** Coursera, Udemy, and edX offer structured coding lessons from beginner to advanced levels.

3. Video Editing

- **Free Tools:** iMovie (Mac users), Descript for basic editing.
- **Paid Tools and Tutorials:** Adobe Premiere Pro and CyberLink PowerDirector with courses available on LinkedIn Learning

Steps to Monetize Your New Skills

- Offer freelance services on platforms like Fiverr or Upwork.
- Create a portfolio showcasing your projects.
- Apply for roles requiring your expertise to secure higher income opportunities.

Conclusion

Upskilling is a vital investment in your future. By leveraging the right mix of resources and staying disciplined, you can master in-demand skills and unlock new income streams.

CHAPTER 21

THE PSYCHOLOGY OF ONLINE SUCCESS

The Role of Mindset in Online Success

Succeeding in the digital space requires more than technical skills—it demands a resilient and adaptive mindset. A growth mindset fosters flexibility, continuous learning, and the ability to thrive under pressure, which are critical for navigating the rapidly evolving online world.

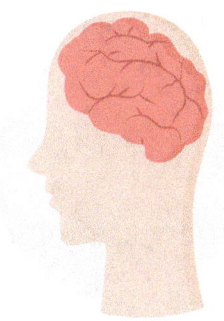

Developing Resilience

- **Embrace Challenges:** View setbacks as opportunities to learn and grow.
- **Practice Self-Care:** Manage stress through regular exercise, mindfulness, and healthy routines.
- **Seek Support:** Build a network of peers and mentors to help navigate difficulties.

Strategies for Continuous Growth

1. Cultivating a Growth Mindset

- **Focus on Learning:** Prioritize skill-building over immediate results.
- **Be Open to Feedback:** Use constructive criticism as a tool for improvement.

2. Staying Motivated

- **Set SMART Goals:** Break long-term objectives into manageable steps.
- **Celebrate Progress:** Recognize small wins to maintain enthusiasm.

3. Building Adaptability

- **Experiment:** Try new strategies and learn from the outcomes.
- **Stay Informed:** Keep up with industry trends to remain competitive.

Conclusion

Success in the online space is a journey of resilience and lifelong growth. By embracing challenges, staying motivated, and continuously evolving, you can unlock your full potential and thrive in any digital venture.

CHAPTER 22

MASTERING ANALYTICS FOR GROWTH

The Role of Analytics in Business Growth

Data analytics is essential for understanding customer behavior, optimizing strategies, and driving growth. Tools like Google Analytics and social media insights empower businesses to make data-driven decisions that enhance performance and profitability.

Key Platforms for Analytics

1. Google Analytics

- **Track User Behavior:** Analyze website traffic, user demographics, and session durations to optimize content and improve user experience.
- **Identify Trends:** Spot high-performing pages and marketing channels.

2. Social Media Insights

- **Understand Engagement:** Measure likes, shares, and comments to refine content strategies.
- **Audience Targeting:** Use data to identify the preferences and behaviors of your social media audience.

3. Advanced Data Tools

- **Visualization Platforms:** Tools like Tableau and Power BI transform raw data into actionable insights.
- **Big Data Solutions:** Use platforms like Hadoop for managing large datasets at scale.

Steps to Leverage Analytics for Growth

- **Define Goals:** Align analytics with business objectives, such as increasing conversion rates or customer retention.
- **Monitor Key Metrics:** Focus on KPIs like bounce rates, click-through rates, and customer acquisition costs.
- **Iterate and Optimize:** Use insights to test and refine strategies for continuous improvement.

Conclusion

Mastering analytics is crucial for scaling any business. By leveraging tools like Google Analytics, social media insights, and advanced data platforms, you can uncover opportunities, streamline operations, and drive sustained growth.

LEGAL AND TAX ADVICE FOR ONLINE EARNERS

The Importance of Legal and Tax Compliance

Freelancers and online entrepreneurs must navigate legal and tax systems to stay compliant, avoid penalties, and optimize earnings. This involves understanding contracts, filing taxes on time, and leveraging tax-saving strategies.

Key Areas to Focus On

1. Tax Compliance

- **Understand Tax Obligations**: Learn about the taxes applicable to your income (e.g., federal, state, or international taxes).
- **Timely Filing**: Use tools like online tax software or consult a professional to ensure accurate and timely tax filing.
- **Track Expenses**: Maintain records of deductions like office supplies, travel costs, and professional services.

2. Contracts and Agreements

- **Draft Clear Contracts:** Include key elements like payment terms, scope of work, and timelines. Contracts protect your rights and set mutual expectations.
- **Seek Legal Advice:** Consult a lawyer to review contracts, especially for long-term or high-value projects.

3. Tax-Saving Tips

- **Claim Deductions:** Deduct business-related expenses, such as internet costs, software subscriptions, and health insurance.
- **Hire Family Members:** Employ family members in your business to reduce taxable income legitimately.
- **Invest in Retirement Plans:** Contribute to retirement savings to lower taxable income while planning for the future.

Steps to Stay Legally Safe and Tax-Efficient

1. **Register Your Business:** If required, choose a business structure (e.g., LLC, sole proprietorship) for liability protection.
2. **Stay Organized:** Use tools to track income, expenses, and tax deadlines.
3. **Plan Ahead:** Set aside a portion of income for taxes to avoid surprises.

Conclusion

Staying legally compliant and tax-savvy is critical for online earners. With clear contracts, proper documentation, and strategic tax planning, freelancers and entrepreneurs can focus on growing their businesses without unnecessary stress.

CHAPTER 24

THE ART OF CROWDFUNDING

What is Crowdfunding?

Crowdfunding is the process of raising small amounts of money from a large number of people, typically via online platforms. It enables creators to bring their ideas to life by harnessing community support.

Popular Crowdfunding Platforms

1. Kickstarter

- **Best For:** Creative projects like art, music, films, and technology.
- **Funding Model:** All-or-nothing—projects must reach their funding goal to receive money.
- **Community Building:** Helps creators engage with supporters and establish a fan base.

2. GoFundMe

- **Best For:** Personal causes, charity, and one-time funding needs.
- **Funding Model:** Flexible funding—creators can access funds even if the target isn't met.
- **Ease of Use:** Ideal for straightforward fundraising campaigns.

Steps to Create a Successful Campaign

1. **Craft a Compelling Story:** Share the vision behind your project with engaging visuals and narratives.
2. **Set a Realistic Goal:** Define clear and achievable funding targets.
3. **Offer Rewards:** Provide exclusive perks like early access, merchandise, or shoutouts for contributors.
4. **Promote Your Campaign:** Use social media, email marketing, and community outreach to amplify visibility.

Benefits of Green Online Ventures

- **Validation:** Helps gauge public interest in your idea before investing heavily.
- **Exposure:** Campaigns on platforms like Kickstarter or GoFundMe attract widespread attention.
- **Community Support:** Builds a loyal audience for future projects.

Conclusion

Crowdfunding is an empowering tool for creators, offering both financial backing and an engaged audience. Platforms like Kickstarter and GoFundMe are gateways to turning creative visions into reality while fostering meaningful connections with supporters.

CHAPTER 25

GREEN ONLINE BUSINESSES

What Are Green Online Businesses?

Green online businesses prioritize environmental sustainability while delivering products or services. They aim to reduce their carbon footprint, promote eco-friendly practices, and address global challenges such as climate change and resource depletion.

Key Principles for Success

1. Triple Bottom Line Approach

- Focus on **people**, **planet**, and **profit** for a balanced, sustainable model.
- Offer products that are ethically sourced and minimize environmental harm.

2. Sustainable Digital Marketing

- Implement low-impact marketing strategies such as email over print and optimize websites to reduce energy consumption.
- Highlight eco-friendly values in branding to resonate with sustainability-conscious customers.

3. Innovative Product Offerings

- Launch eco-conscious goods or services like green tech apps, digital consulting for sustainability, or recyclable packaging options.

Steps to Build a Green Online Business

1. Assess Sustainability Goals: Identify areas to minimize waste and energy use.
2. Choose Ethical Suppliers: Partner with vendors that share eco-friendly values.
3. Engage Customers: Promote transparency by sharing efforts like carbon offset programs or eco-certifications.
4. Leverage Technology: Use cloud computing to reduce physical infrastructure and opt for digital products to cut material waste.

Benefits of Green Online Ventures

- **Increased Loyalty:** Consumers support businesses that reflect their values.
- **Market Differentiation:** Eco-friendly strategies make businesses stand out in competitive markets.
- **Long-Term Savings:** Energy-efficient operations reduce costs over time.

Conclusion

Green online businesses succeed by aligning economic goals with sustainable practices. They contribute to solving global challenges while creating resilient, impactful ventures that resonate with environmentally conscious customers.

CHAPTER 26

SUCCESS STORIES FROM ONLINE ENTREPRENEURS

Why Success Stories Matter

Learning from successful online entrepreneurs provides valuable insights into overcoming challenges, leveraging opportunities, and staying resilient. These stories serve as roadmaps for those navigating their digital ventures.

Inspiring Online Entrepreneurs

1. Jeff Bezos – Amazon

What began as an online bookstore in Jeff Bezos' garage evolved into the world's largest eCommerce platform. His focus on customer obsession and innovation transformed Amazon into a household name. Key lessons include prioritizing user experience and reinvesting profits into growth.

2. Sophia Amoruso – Nasty Gal

Sophia started selling vintage clothing on eBay, eventually turning her passion into Nasty Gal, a multi-million-dollar online fashion retailer. Her story highlights the power of identifying a niche and building a strong personal brand.

3. Steve Jobs & Steve Wozniak – Apple

From a humble garage setup, the founders turned Apple into a tech giant through relentless innovation. Their story emphasizes the importance of vision, adaptability, and perseverance.

Jeff Bezos – Amazon

Steve Jobs

Sophia Amoruso

Key Takeaways

- Innovate Relentlessly: Embrace new ideas and technologies to stay ahead.
- Understand Your Market: Focus on customer needs and market gaps.
- Build a Brand: Establish a unique identity that resonates with your audience.
- Stay Resilient: Persevere through challenges and adapt to changing conditions.

Conclusion

The success of these entrepreneurs highlights the opportunities available in the digital landscape. Whether it's eCommerce, tech, or personal branding, their journeys inspire aspiring entrepreneurs to dream big and act strategically.

CHAPTER 27

RECOVERING FROM FAILURES

Embracing Failure as a Learning Opportunity

Failure is not the end but a stepping stone in the entrepreneurial journey. By examining the reasons behind setbacks, you can identify mistakes and transform them into growth opportunities.

Strategies for Recovering from Failures

1. Analyze and Reflect

Take a step back to review what went wrong. Was it a product-market mismatch? Poor timing? Ineffective marketing? Pinpointing the root cause helps ensure you don't repeat the same mistakes.

2. Learn and Adapt

Failures are rich with lessons. For example, use customer feedback to refine your offerings or shift to a more viable market segment.

3. Celebrate Small Wins

Counter the negativity of setbacks by acknowledging incremental progress. This boosts morale and builds momentum for recovery.

Effective Pivoting

1. Reevaluate Your Goals

Sometimes, a new direction aligns better with your skills and market needs. Shifting focus doesn't mean abandoning your vision—it means adapting to reality.

2. Innovate with Resilience

Use insights from failures to innovate. For instance, a failed e-Commerce site could pivot into a niche subscription model targeting a loyal customer base.

Key Takeaways

- Treat failure as a teacher.
- Pivot strategically, using setbacks as a source of clarity.
- Stay resilient and focused on long-term growth.

CONCLUSION

Staying Adaptable

Adapting to trends, continuously learning, and preparing for the future of the digital economy.

Balancing Online Work and Life

Maintaining a healthy work-life balance through time management and mental well-being practices.